P9-ARK-216

FROM THE STREETS TO THE STAGE

20 Ways to make it from the Streets of your Fears to the Stage of your Dreams

Monti Washington

PRAISE FOR MONTI'S STREETS TO THE STAGE

Monti's Book is a must read for all youth and anyone who works with today's youth . Monti's life is compelling and liberating. Thank you Monti for being so candid and transparent in your writings. Many lives will be transformed for the better, because you had the courage to write this remarkable book!

Monti Washington is an incredible example that you must live your life without excuses. Thank you Monti for teaching our youth that you should never let your past predict your future! Monti Washington not only played in the park, he lived in the park as well. Thank you Monti for having the mindset to persevere. You have not only given us hope, but you have given us the tools to win in life. Through your life many youth have been given hope and a practical formula to go from the streets of their fears to the stage of their dreams! Thank you for being a living example of how to turn adversity into success!

Jerome Vincent Carter, speaker, author, former college professor
www.inspiration52.com

"Monti Washington peels back the layers of hurt in his life so that we may benefit from his experience. This is a sacrifice many who are privileged like myself take for granted. Not only has our privilege created oppression, but now we expect those who experience it to teach us something without asking. Monti's selflessness is a gift and he has taken it upon himself to teach, inspire and motivate anyone willing to listen or read what he has to offer. His story reflects something in all of us. The difference is that he is allowing us to learn from it. I suggest we take that opportunity."

Michael Sliwa, speaker, author, and educator for 25 years

"His uplifting story combined with the 20 lessons from this book makes this book a must read for anyone wanting to know how to succeed through their challenges. "

Hardy Brown, San Bernardino County Superintendent of Schools

"As a pro athlete I deal with adversity every game and on every play. Monti's book teaches people how to turn adversity into Super Bowl type success."

Prince Amukamara, Super Bowl Champion of the New York Giants

"Monti Washington has decoded the guise of success with *Success starts with Adversity*. This practical tool equips foster youth with information to transform their pain into power and assist them in creating the life of their dreams rather than settling within the odds they've been dealt."

Franco O. Vega
Executive Director/Founder of the Right Way Foundation

"After being openly struck by a speeding car at the age of 3 and subsequently being brought back life, I spent 3 months in traction in the hospital and almost an entire year in a body cast. When I read Monti's story I was truly moved by not only the parallels of our childhood traumas, but even more so how he chose to RESPOND and become more than the circumstances he was in. If this book doesn't want to make you strap on a CAPE and soar to new heights in your life, then you will probably want to seek medical attention for having no pulse! Monti embodies what being a superhero is all about."

TW Walker

Personal Development Trainer | Author of Superhero Success | Consultant

www.TWWalker.com

It has been an amazing experience to watch Monti Washington grow over the past ten years! I am extremely excited about his book! When I first saw Monti in action, he was the most relatable and effective speaker I had ever seen work with young people who were struggling to overcome obstacles. As I have had the opportunity to continue to observe Monti interact with all types of people at all ages, my respect for him has grown. I have been fortunate as a school administrator to bring Monti to speak with and mentor young people in every school and environment that I have worked. My only frustration was that the demand for his services exceeds his availability. This book is an answer to that problem, providing others with real-life strategies to overcome obstacles and find their success. This book is a written version of what Monti offers in person - a relatable and effective approach to achieving personal goals regardless of the obstacles people face. I will use this book in my work to support young people!

Amy Perhamus, Education Consultant, 30 year educator

Copyright

No part of this book may be duplicated, reproduced, or transmitted in any form or means, electronic, or mechanical, including photocopying, recording, or by any information, storage, or retrieval system without the written permission from the publisher.

Copyright © 2015 by Monti Washington

All rights reserved. This book or any portion thereof may not be reproduced or used in any manner whatsoever without the express written permission of the publisher except for the use of brief quotations in a book review.

Printed in the United States of America

First Printing, 2015

ISBN 978-1-4951-6279-4

Monti Washington
5000 Woodman Ave Suite. 11
Sherman Oaks, CA, 91423

www.Montivation.com

TABLE OF CONTENTS

Dedication

There are a number of people that I wish to dedicate this book to who have had a great impact on my journey. Everyone from the teachers who helped me along the way to the people who worked in the group homes where I lived to the mentors I have now. But more than anyone I would like to thank the person who is the greatest source of my pain and struggle which have lead me to my success today. I would like to dedicate this book to my biological mother, Shontia Washington.

Mom, your actions have had a domino effect on my life that led to my abuse, suffering, confusion, and my evolving sense of self-worth. The choices you made in your personal life impacted me in ways that will last a lifetime. The pain I have carried all these years coupled with the anger inside of me has left me empty with no way to fill up. No matter my feelings toward you, the fact remains that you are my mother. That is why I forgive you. I forgive you for every mistake that you made in your life that impacted my life negatively. I forgive you for abandoning me and my younger siblings. I forgive you for leaving me at a park for weeks at a time. I forgive you for allowing me to be put into foster homes and suffer abuse. Not only do I forgive you but I thank you!

Everything that I experienced has made me who I am today. My suffering, once a weight that held me down, is now my greatest source of strength. My pain can now be transformed into inspiration to help others. Without you I doubt I would have been able to find my purpose in life so quickly. So I thank you, mother, from the innermost part of my soul. I love you. Even though you may never read this, even though I may never see you or speak to you again, know that I love you.

Foreward

The first time I saw Monti Washington walk into a room I wasn't ready for it. I could immediately sense a pureness and joy fleeting from his boastful smile; a genuine love for life that I just couldn't understand any human being having at the time.

Since that day, nearly ten years ago, Monti has exuded that same desire to embrace and embody all of the beautiful things living life wholeheartedly entails. I have never met another human being who shines as much light into any room, however big or dark, as he does. Anyone who has been in the same vicinity as him can attest to this.

As someone who has had the privilege of being there to witness his character both develop and be tested on nearly every level imaginable throughout the years, I can testify that his courageous spirit to stay positive through nearly every difficult circumstance never falters. He not only epitomizes perseverance, but he takes it a step further and embodies the true heart of inspiration.

For most people who have had the honor of hearing even a small part of Monti's story, you probably wouldn't understand how he could be as genuinely positive about life as he is. If you have ever seen firsthand the streets that he has actually laid his head on at night, or the tears he forces back when the topics of particular family members arise, you would never imagine that through every dark alley, his bare and blistered feet have wondered, he never ceases to shine light. Even more, he is the first person to pick up any one else along the way and help to encourage them to keep moving forward as well.

I'll never forget the day when Monti took a few friends of ours and I on a journey to visit the streets of where he grew up. As he took us through a day in his shoes I watched as his innate survival skills kicked in (he was much more composed then we were). He walked us through the areas where there were crack houses his mom would stay in, the convenience stores he begged for money outside of, and the streets and parks he slept in. What shocked me most though, was watching him only a few days later when he was back on stage inspiring thousands of students through their personal walks in life. It was then I knew that he had a rare, and innate, ability to use his pain for a greater purpose to serve others.

Monti's fighting spirit to overcome every obstacle and adversity that stands in between him and his potential is nothing short of inspiring and to an extent, miraculous. His energy speaks right down to the core of the human heart and whether you are ready for it or not, it will make you want to stand right beside him and, together, fight for that person buried deep inside of you that you were always meant to become. Whether he is performing on stage as an actor or as an artist at a slam poetry event or when he is speaking life into thousands of students' lives, his energy is always magnetic.

Monti Washington not only brings out the best in every person I have ever seen him encounter, including myself, he reminds us all what it truly means to defy all odds and live a life so passionately that we can't help but believe anything is truly possible.

Julia Garcia is a top female motivational speaker and bestselling author who has gone on to create and co-found the non-profit organization "The TRU Movement" - an organization that uses motivational speaking through the arts to empower youth nation-wide.

INTRODUCTION

From birth, my life has been filled with one heartbreaking obstacle after another. I was conceived in a hotel room, a product of a one-night stand. I have never met my biological father and I doubt he even knows I exist. My mother has been on drugs for as long as I can remember. Even now I have very few memories of her sober and drug free. I can recall the look on my mother's face the first time I saw her smoke crack cocaine.

Her eyes were rolling in the back of her head as though she was already dead. She had a blank look on her face like she didn't know where she was. Physically she was sitting in front of me but mentally she was somewhere else where her own kids did not exist. The stale smell of cocaine permeated the entire room, making it hard to breath. That smell still haunts my senses to this day. But what's more haunting is the memory of my mother's reaction the first time we were taken out of her custody. I recall the loud knock on the door followed by these words "This is the police open up." When my mother answered the door the cops knew the situation immediately. Apparently a neighbor knew what was going on in my home long before I knew my mother was addicted to drugs.

As the cops entered our house and saw the filth and unlivable conditions, I could see the look of discomfort on my mother's face. As they searched the house I remember just sitting there in fear. Although the abuse of drugs was a fairly new concept to me, I have seen far too many people I love hauled off to jail. As they put handcuffs on my mother a sudden rush of intense fear overcame me. My mother, with no tears in her eyes and only a glazed over look, was put in the back of a cop car and was taken away.

Why was mom going to jail? What could she have possibly done wrong? Before my next thought I found myself sitting in the back of a cop car. Although the officers did their best to make me feel comfortable in the situation, I'll never forget that feeling. I was all but sure that I was being hauled off to prison. That was until I arrived at a house in the middle of the night somewhere across town. This would

be the first time I learned what a group home was, separated from my
two younger brothers that I had grown accustomed to taking care of.
They were was no longer by my side. So there I was, scared and alone
in a place I have never known.

Although that was the first time I saw her abuse drugs and the first time we were taken from her, it would not be the last. So began my rough cycle of abuse, neglect, and aloneness.

I dealt with a great deal of adversity growing up in poverty. I have lived in countless homeless shelters and group homes. Cramped in large rooms filled with strangers with nothing more than a change of clothes and a pillow was normal for me. Living constantly in awkward and uncomfortable situations where I had to overcome adversity to survive, only to later find yourself in the even more uncomfortable position of sleeping in parks for weeks on end. That left me wondering why the other kids get play at the park and return home, while you played at the park and called it home.

The most difficult times were those spent in foster homes. My very first foster parent physically abused me and my two younger brothers. As a kid, I had what you would call "sticky fingers". Growing up on the streets, I developed the habit of stealing often. Unfortunately, I took that habit into my first foster home. My foster mom would beat me in a very specific and creative way every time I stole something. She would make me grip the back of a dining room chair with my knuckles exposed. She would then get a metal hanger and hit my knuckles until they began to bleed or until she felt I learned my lesson. Eventually my younger brothers and I were removed from that home, but because of her abuse, my hands were shaky and unsteady for years.

In my second foster home I was emotionally and mentally abused. The moment we arrived I felt an overwhelming sense of security. It was a beautiful house in a neighborhood around the corner from this lake I loved to visit. There were none of the shootings, yelling, liquor stores, or dirt fields that I had become accustomed to. After a couple of months that feeling was replaced with depression. I was consumed with an empty feeling of not belonging and not wanting to live. For three months I was locked in the back room of the home for 23 hours a day with little to no light. There was no reason my foster mother gave me and my brothers for treating us this way other than, "You ain't shit."

Being called dumb and told you're nothing while being locked in a dark room all day is adversity at its core. I was at one of the lowest points in my life at only 12 years old when I tried to commit suicide. After being treated that way by parent after parent, I didn't see the point in living anymore. Luckily, ending my life was not something I was very good at. But, at the time, the reality of the adversity I was faced with was far too great for me to handle. I had no idea that even in situations as bad as that it was possible for me to turn adversity into success.

Handling the emotional strain of being told, "you aint shit" time and time again, while being locked in a dark room for 23 hours a day, combined with the psychological issues you get living and seeing what I saw growing up, prepared me for any obstacle I can face today. Even dealing with the mental scars created from being told how dumb you are, forcing you to be in special education classes up until high school all prepared me for the trials of everyday life. I have made it **FROM THE STREETS TO THE STAGE AND HAVE LEARNED HOW TO TURN ADVERSITY INTO SUCCESS!**

Self-help is what I believe to be the single most important area of study necessary to gain lasting success. Having mentors, a community, and people who uplift you are all good and well, but you have to have the desire to want better for yourself. What I have gained from these experiences has allowed me to create a list of tips to allow you to make it from the streets of your fears to the stage of your dreams. Ultimately, allowing you to turn Adversity into Success. These tips will encourage, motivate, and educate you on how to take all the negativity you go through in life and use it to build you up instead of breaking you down. You will learn how not to let the adversity in your life destroy you but instead drive you to achieve more in life! If you apply them to your everyday life then you will make it from the streets of your fears to the stage of your dreams while learning how to turn adversity into success!

CHAPTER 1

WHY ME

(Know you're why)

CHAPTER 1

WHY ME? (Know Your Why)

"Be flexible about how you do things, but inflexible about why you do things." –Thomas Blackwell

Growing up there were a few questions that I found myself always asking. "Why me? Why is my mother on drugs? Why don't I have a father? Why am I poor? Why me?" It's a question many of us have asked at one point or another in our lives. Not knowing the answer to that question can keep you wondering the rest of your life, leaving you to question everything in your life.

"Why?", is the single most important question we can ask ourselves in life. Knowing the answer to "why?" is what helps define our purpose. It helps us get to the root of any problem we have. There are times in life when we don't have any sort of answer or solution to the adversity we're facing. It is in these moments we want to give up and throw in the towel. This is when your "why?" is most important. Your "why?" is that extra 10% when you've given your 100%. It is the reserve tank when you've run out of gas. Your "why?" is what will get you through the toughest spots in your life.

There was a young man who was born with dwarfism, was in a wheelchair, and was also blind, that I had the pleasure of meeting while speaking once. His name was Rich, but I nicked named him "Richie Rich". One of the activities I like doing when I speak is to ask people from the audience "what one word would you use to describe yourself?" It's very interesting to see what words people use because you never really know just by looking at people. But when I asked him to tell me one word to describe himself, he told me, "UNSTOPPABLE". My breath was taken away. I then asked him, "Why do you feel you have to be unstoppable?" He said because he has to be the role model to his little brothers and sister. Here is this young man with every justifiable reason to give up on life, but he refuses to because he needs to be a role model for his younger siblings. His "why?" are his siblings. It's such a strong reason that despite being blind and in a wheelchair, he still feels unstoppable.

FIND YOUR "WHY?" Find a reason so strong that there are no obstacles strong enough in the world to stop you. This "why" needs to be something that affects you emotionally every time you think of it. It can be a dream, family member, loved one who passed away, anything that gives you the strength to move forward. The key is to choose this "why" from an emotional standpoint. Money, cars, or big houses are rarely strong enough reasons to make it through extreme situations. Your "why" should make you feel unstoppable when you think about it!

CHAPTER 2

WHY IS THEIR GRASS GREENER

(Focus, People, Focus.)

CHAPTER 2

WHY IS THEIR GRASS GREENER THAN OURS... (Focus, People, Focus.)

"Don't dwell on what went wrong; instead focus on what to do next." –Denis Waitley

I have always had this bad habit of comparing my life to others in every situation. I was always comparing what little I had to how much someone else had. It kept me in a place of fear, insecurity, and more often than not, jealousy. I would be jealous of friends who had better clothes, both parents, a house to live in, and anyone who had more than I did. I forgot that no matter how bad I had it there was always someone worse off. What you call a curse someone else considers a blessing.

Don't compare your "chapter one" with someone else's "chapter twenty." To put it simply people, WE DON'T LOOK OUR STORY! When we look at all the material wealth and success someone has, we don't know how long it took them to get there. We are unaware of each step and fall along the way. We only see the rewards in the light of day, but are unaware of failures in the dark of night! There are truly no overnight success stories no matter what you may have heard. We must remember that we rarely know what someone is truly feeling inside. As an actor and a motivational speaker, I often hear stories about celebrities committing suicide. They turn to a life of sex, drugs, and alcohol to numb the pain that others don't see on the surface.

The grass is always greener on the other side if you're not watering your own grass. When you're going through hard times, it's easy to look at someone else's life and think they have it easier. You assume that they have absolutely no problem in the world. But the fact is that we never really know what someone else did to make their grass green.

When we are so focused on the success of others we forget how far we have come ourselves. By doing this we unknowingly discourage ourselves from continuing toward success. We focus on what we don't have rather than what we *do* have. We focus on everything that is going wrong in our lives rather than what's right. In essence, we forget to water our own grass, which leaves it looking worse than other lawns around us.

Focus helps us transform adversity into anything we choose. People who can focus for long periods of time achieve more than those who can't. It's important to focus on the solution to our problems and not the problems themselves. The less distracted you are, the more you can get done. That is why people who have goals and focus on a particular direction in their lives find greater success than most. Whatever you focus on most in your life you'll start seeing often!

FOCUS EVERYTHING YOU HAVE ON ONE PARTICULAR GOAL. It can be to get better grades, be in a healthy relationship, get that internship secured, get your own place, or get in the best shape of your life. **For the next month I want you to focus on ways to improve that area and everyday take action on making it better.** Let your mind think of every possible way to achieve the goal without limiting yourself. Write it down where you will see it everyday. You should read it when you go to bed and when you wake up in the morning. You want to create the habit of focusing on this one goal. At the end of the month you will be surprised at how much you're able to accomplish with 100% of your focus. You will not worry about how green someone else's grass is, because you'll have the best lawn on the block.

CHAPTER 3

STICKS AND STONES

(Power of Words)

CHAPTER 3

STICKS AND STONES... (Power of Words)

"Truth is nothing... What you believe to be true is everything."
–Anonymous

I was called stupid so many times by my second foster parents that it became part of who I was. Day after day they told me that I was stupid, called me stupid, and often reminded me of how stupid I was with every mistake I made. I was called stupid so much that I thought it was my name. It had become part of my belief system. It stunted my growth and made me suicidal. The effect of words on us can last a lifetime and even shape our lives. In my case, sticks and stones may break bones, but words nearly killed me.

I spent many days contemplating suicide while in my second foster home. Being confined to a dark room while being torn apart mentally and emotionally was rough. It made me not want to live anymore. I would imagine how to hang myself, how many pills it would take to kill me, and how free I would feel. Fortunately for me, at the height of my depression, my younger brothers and I were taken from that foster home and placed in a better situation.

Sticks and stones break bones but words leave scars! Words carry enormous power that has a lasting effect. Often these words are said when we're vulnerable and by someone whose words mean the most to us. We give an overwhelming amount of power to thoughts that come from the mouth of someone trying to harm us. It's important to understand that their words are just words! They hold us down only as long as we allow them to.

The right words can bring encouragement, energy, and empowerment into our daily lives. The wrong ones can confine you to a mental prison that's nearly impossible to escape. The feelings associated with negative words can cripple us for as long as we allow it. This is why we must be careful about what we say and

what we listen to. Someone once told me, that "we are what we think." If we're not careful, we can also become what others think.

GIVE THE RIGHT WORDS POWER! Use words that empower you every time you speak them. Phrases such as "I can't", "I give up", "I didn't think", "I'm afraid of", "It's impossible", and "I don't believe" are words that steal power. Have "**POWER WORDS**" and "**SUCCESS PHRASES**" such as, "I expect", "I believe", "it's possible", or "I'll find a way!" Allow the words you use to empower you to accomplish incredible feats. In his book "**ASPIRE**" Kevin Hall talks about the immense power of words. He writes about. "Ollin," pronounced "all in," which means to "move and act now with all your heart." It's a powerful word that I try to use in everyday life. Learn to use these words to replace those that steal your energy. Remember that sticks and stones may break bones, but words leaves scars.

CHAPTER 4

F.L.Y

(First Love Yourself)

CHAPTER 4

F.L.Y... (First Love Yourself)

"Never be bullied into silence. Never allow yourself to be made a victim. Accept no one's definition of your life, but define yourself."
–Harvey Fierstein

As I mentioned before, there was a point in my young life where I had absolutely no love for myself. I had no concern for my future or well-being. I had been emotionally and mentally scared to the point that I no longer wanted to live. Being trapped in a dark room for 23 hours a day took away all hope I had for a better life. I genuinely felt that the world would be a better place if I was not around. If my foster mom did not walk into the room at the time that she did, you would not be reading this book. Thankfully, I learned how to F.L.Y.

Far too many people look for love outside themselves. I saw my mother get involved in many unhealthy relationships and witnessed her believe that the abuse she suffered was a sign of love. I have witnessed young women on Instagram and Facebook get depressed because they didn't get enough likes. Every year we hear about some celebrity who has died of a drug overdose or suicide. There are countless examples of people seeking validation outside themselves because they lack love for themselves.

Attention is not love. Compliments and praise are not love. Love is a light inside of you that shines outwardly for others to see. It has to start inside you before anyone else can see it. Searching for love outside yourself is a temporary solution to a permanent problem. Kanye West writes in a song, "I could be by myself and enjoy the company." I love that line because beneath the cocky exterior there is truth to what he said. If you can't love yourself wouldn't it be hard for someone else to? Love is a reflection of the self-esteem and confidence you already have. There is not enough make-up, clothes, or money to substitute for the beauty of loving yourself first.

When you F.L.Y the sky is not your limit, only your capacity to love is. Your insecurities and doubts no longer weigh you down, keeping you on the ground. The heights of your success will be largely determined by how well you can F.L.Y. It is your responsibility to find even the smallest reason to love yourself first. It can be a challenge to be alone and discover the love that is already inside you. Especially if you have suffered the level of abuse that I have, finding that "something" to love about yourself is like finding a needle in a haystack on top of a haystack filled with needles. Just like air, even though you can't see it, believe me it's there.

FIRST LOVE YOURSELF: Before you can F.L.Y you have to discover why you're stuck on the ground. Ask yourself, "What is holding me back?" It could be that no one has ever taught you how to love yourself. It could be because of a traumatic past that has robbed you of it. YOU ARE NOT A HELPLESS VICTIM! There are no excuses for not loving yourself. I'm not saying that it's going to be easy, but it's necessary. It's necessary for you to take back the power you're entitled to that comes with loving oneself. You'll face a lot of disappointment along the way, but you should never quit. Believe me, when you're able to F.L.Y, you'll simply be able to rise above all the hardships thrown at you. But **FIRST LOVE YOURSELF**.

CHAPTER 5

KETCHUP, PLEASE

(See Your Past Differently)

CHAPTER 5

KETCHUP, PLEASE ... (See Your Past Differently)

"Study the past if you would define the future." –Confucius

Remembering how hard my childhood was always keeps me motivated. At the height of my mother's drug addiction, we lived in the ghetto in projects that made a third world country look like the Hilton. Over half of the apartments were abandoned and boarded up; the rest were infested with cockroaches and often had no electricity. Our apartment smelled of dirt and desperation. While living there, my mother would abandon me and my younger brothers for days on end. Trapped in her desperate pursuit of drugs, she would often forget she even had kids. She would always say, "I'll be back, ya'll be good and don't get into any trouble." As young as I was, I knew what this really meant.

While my mother was away, there would be no food in the house. We would go down to the closest fast food restaurant and beg for money or steal food. We usually stole the easiest available item which was ketchup packages. They were small, free, and easy to conceal. Shoving as many into our pockets as we could before getting caught, we would take them home and squeeze each packet into our mouths. We savored every last drop until there was nothing left but a packet as empty as our refrigerator. Sometimes, if we were lucky, we would get a loaf of bread and make a "ketchup sandwich". Surprisingly despite the lack of meat, vegetables, or any typical sandwich fixings, it made for an almost satisfying meal (not really). Truth be told, the ketchup was usually all we had.

Remembering what we have overcome and how far we have come, keeps us focused on our goals. It's not always what you achieve that gives you the confidence to pursue your dreams, but what you've overcome. Too often we are enslaved to our past, seeing our pain as something that has held us back rather than something that can uplift us. Remembering those packages of ketchup makes me so very grateful for every meal I now have.

Ketchup to your past: Think back to a tough time in your life. Maybe it was an life-changing injury, your parents' divorce, a lack of money, issues with close friends, or self-esteem issues. Now think about how that made you feel. Does it bring you down? Does it fill you with regret? If it does, look at it from a different perspective. See it as something you survived, overcame, defeated, rather than something that has held you back. Our past is how we see it. You can see your struggles as a disadvantage or an advantage. Ketchup to your past! Go backwards to move forward! Recalling those tough times allows you to see what was holding you back from having the present and future that you want. The key is to reflect **NOT** dwell on the past.

My friends always laugh at me because I always carry a ketchup package in my pocket. The ketchup package in my pocket that I carry every day is a reminder of what I have overcome. What is your Ketchup package? What do you have that can remind you just how strong you really are? What do you have that reminds you of just how powerful and amazing you really are? Take a picture of it, keep a memory of it, or, if possible, carry it with you. Life is always changing and we never know what is coming our way. When our present looks bad, and our dreams look impossible, we have our past to remind us just how far we have come. **Ketchup** to your past only to **relish** in the moment!

CHAPTER 6

WHEN LIFE GIVES YOU LEMONS

(Create Your Own Opportunity)

CHAPTER 6

WHEN LIFE GIVES YOU LEMONS...
(Create Your Own Opportunity)

"See the opportunity in every obstacle" – Anonymous

There was a time in my life when I was sleeping on cardboard boxes and had to create an opportunity for myself rather than just waiting for one. I turned thrown-away cardboard boxes into enough money to feed myself and two younger brothers for an entire summer. That one experience allowed me to see the opportunity in every situation moving forward in my life. I began to embrace any challenge I engaged in almost immediately looking for the opportunity in the midst of the difficulty. I didn't know it but I was a young entrepreneur.

When life gives you lemons don't make lemonade. Instead plant the seeds, grow a tree, and sell back the lemons to life and make some money out of it. In other words, become an entrepreneur as soon as possible. Entrepreneurship is one of the most important skills you'll ever learn. There are now so many opportunities to make money that you would be a fool not to take advantage of what's available. With the Internet and social media so easily accessible, the ability to make a name for yourself is just a click away. Right now 20 year old college senior Marques Brownlee reviews tech products on YouTube. Through advertising on his YouTube channel, he earns anywhere from $117,000 to $934,000 a year! The guy is not even out of college yet! With nothing more than a camera in his room he has been able to take advantage of the opportunity that YouTube has presented. If you were to ask, he would tell you that he had many setbacks along the way.

Entrepreneurship forces you to deal consistently with adversity. You learn to turn life's obstacles into opportunities for your benefit and your growth. The excitement, independence, flexibility, and freedom of living life on your own terms is an amazing feeling.

Having my own speaking business, I can attest to the freedom and excitement I have. Has it been hard? Yes! Has it been difficult? Yes! But it has also been worth every single disappointment and setback along the way. Life had given me sour lemons time and time again. Growing up in poverty and enduring abuse were very sour lemons indeed. But I took those lemons and turned it into a business where I get to positively influence people's lives.

BECOME AN ENTREPRENEUR! Life will give you many lemons, each one with that sour taste. You can choose to make lemonade out of it and simply turn it into a lesson. Or, you can take the lessons and turn it into something **more.** Turn it into something that will benefit you and others for the rest of your life. There is an opportunity in every difficulty. Our world desperately needs problem-solvers and creative people with minds like yours. Ask yourself, "What problems am I good at solving?" "Who else has these problems?" And, "How can I solve their problems?" When you become great at solving problems for people, they will pay you for it! Not only are you helping them, but you are helping yourself in the process. Remember that all adversity works for-you, not against you. Your struggles, challenges, and adversity are all a way for you to have more opportunities to progress.

CHAPTER 7

PLAY THE CARDS YOU'RE GIVEN

(Circumstances)

CHAPTER 7

PLAY THE CARDS YOU'RE GIVEN... (Circumstances)

"Each player must accept the cards dealt to him ..." Francois Voltaire

If my childhood was a poker hand, I literally would have an empty house rather than a full house. I was dealt a horrible hand in this game called life. Every disadvantage there was, I had. The cards were definitely not stacked in my favor being that I was homeless and suffered every type of abuse. My confidence needed a search party, my self-esteem needed a makeover, and any thought of a positive future for me did not exist. I finally learned that you are dealt many unfair cards in life, but it's how you play them that mean the most!

Life is not fair! You've heard it, I've heard it, we have all heard it! Now I really hate to break it to you, but it's true! Some of us are born to unfit parents, born with disorders, some of us are born in countries without the opportunities the United States has. Regardless of how unfair your life may be, you always have a choice of how to play the cards you're dealt.

The difficulty we face is often unfair, but only if you don't play your cards right. By looking at every adversity as an opportunity to get better, learn, and progress, you come closer to that success you've always wanted. But when you see misfortune as unfair, you slowly give up your power to change it to your benefit. You are allowing something **that can strengthen you to instead weaken you**. Remember that even a poker player who is dealt a bad hand can still win the game!

MAKE THE DEALER RESHUFFLE! From now on, accept nothing but the best. Do not settle for less when you know you deserve more. Whether it's a job, relationship, friendship, or the relationship with yourself! Create a mindset that allows you to play every hand you are dealt to the best of your ability. When you feel like you are being treated unfairly, speak up! When you feel you can do more, then do more! Demand of yourself the best life has to offer. When you learn how to convert adversity into success, you will no longer have to play any cards you're dealt. You'll be in a position to make the dealer reshuffle and give you the cards you want!

CHAPTER 8

LOL

(Shut up and laugh)

CHAPTER 8

L.O.L... (Shut up and laugh)

"Worry does not empty tomorrow of its sorrow. It empties today of its strength." – Corrie Ten Boom

As a kid, I was constantly in situations that were out of my control. Having no father around and a mother who struggled with drugs left me in "lose-lose" situations. Often the only choice I had was how I chose to look at my situation. I could be depressed or look at things from a positive perspective. In most cases I chose to look at things from a positive perspective and put a positive spin on things. I developed a great sense of humor during my childhood that I still have. Life can be very ironic and unpredictable. It's important to step back and simply laugh at our life, especially when were overwhelmed.

When things go wrong we often think of the worst possible outcome. The moment adversity hits us, our minds go through every possibility even if it's highly unlikely to happen. For example: Traffic is bad so you are 10 minutes late to the final exam. You think the teacher will not let you take the test, causing you to fail the course and be you short on credits for class. Now you can't graduate college but have to pay back your loans. Since you didn't graduate you have to get a minimum wage job. Now you can't afford the big house and BMW, which forces you to settle. No one wants to marry someone who is broke, so you'll never have true love with that supermodel. At times like these we need a **MENTAL TIMEOUT INSTEAD OF A MENTAL BREAKDOWN.** Albert Einstein said, "We cannot solve our problems with same level of thinking that created them." How can we follow Einstein's advice if were thinking about the worst possible outcome? It's impossible! We have to take a step back and see the problem for what it is and not for what we make it out to be.

LAUGH OUT LOUD.   When you're faced with a situation that is out of your control, just laugh out loud. Laugh, giggle, snicker, do whatever you have to do to PRESS THE PAUSE BUTTON ON YOUR THOUGHTS. Sometimes things get so messed up and out of our control that we have no choice but to laugh! In that moment being stressed out or panicking will only make things worse. By laughing out loud you are telling your mind and body to calm down and just relax. You are altering your mental and physical state which allows you to see the problem for what it is and not what you make it to be. Watch something funny on YouTube that makes absolutely no sense! No matter how ridiculous it may sound, laugh your butt off! When you feel better, you will see the situation for what it is and not what you make it to be.

CHAPTER 9

JUST LIKE EVERYONE ELSE

(Why Settle for Average)

CHAPTER 9

JUST LIKE EVERYONE ELSE... (Why Settle for Average)

"You can't blend in and stand out at the same time" – Anonymous

I have always been what my friends call, "a weird person." I take it as a compliment all day long! In high school I was the jock that guys looked up to and that the girls wanted to date. At the same time I was a theater geek, an Anime freak, and was always the guy hanging out with a different group of people! I had no crew or clique that I would only associate with during that time in high school where you had to "belong" to fit in. I was and still am a very curious guy who loves variety in all forms. This, of course, goes against the saying "Birds of a feather flock together." I HAD A BUNCH OF DIFFERENT FEATHERS! Because of my natural ability to be myself, I have always stood out from the crowd. In fact, I always went against what was popular, cool, the trend, and what was accepted. I have always felt that trying to be like everyone else is an insult to myself. I was created to be unique and one of a kind so why not live my life that way?

Trying to be yourself in a world that wants you to be like everyone else is very difficult. There is a lot of adversity that comes with choosing to stand out and rise above the influence. Being an "average" person allows you to blend in and get accepted easier by your peers. It's no wonder why so many people succumb to peer pressure and settle into a life of mediocrity they have created for themselves. **YOU WERE BORN UNIQUE AND AWESOME!**

People who choose to be average limit their own potential. When you try to be like most people, you end up like most people. Average! By definition, the majority of people in life fall into the category of "average." Some excel and are considered above average (where you want to be). Some fall below and are considered below average (where you never want to be). Your potential is so far above average that you need a plane to reach it. The truth is that it takes no effort or growth on your part to be average. What if you gave your best performance and someone said, "Your performance was average" ? What if, after you got dressed to go, you asked your date "How do I look?", and your date said, "About average, baby." Wouldn't that make you feel well, um, I don't know, terrible? **NO ONE LIKES TO BE CALLED AVERAGE, BUT PEOPLE DO THINGS EVERY DAY TO REMAIN AVERAGE.** Greatness and average cannot coexist.

You were born to be one of a kind. The chances of you being born on the day you were born, at the exact same time, with the exact DNA structure, to the exact same parents are 1:400,000,000,000. A one in four hundred billion chance of that happening. So why are you afraid of being yourself? I hate to break it you but **YOU DON'T REALLY HAVE MUCH OF A CHOICE.** It's so much harder trying to be something you're not than being who you are. Embrace yourself and all the struggles that come along with it.

BE A LOVER NOT A FIGHTER! I know what you're thinking, "Excuse me tall, bald, black man, what do you mean be a lover not a fighter? When people love what they do, they normally excel at it. The dancer will practice nine hours a day until she gets a move down. An aspiring doctor will attend school for 10 years or more just earn the title of doctor. An Olympic sprinter will train six hours a day for four years, all for a 10 second race. When you love what you do, it hurts to be average. It hurts not to be the best after all of your hard work. On the other hand, when you do things you don't like, you fight it. You fight getting to that class you hate. You fight getting out of bed for the job that you truly dislike. When you Love what you do, you don't have to worry or even consider being average. They enjoy the challenge and every adversity that comes their way. Doing what you love prevents you from being average because most people don't do what they love. They do what "most" people do: settle and find comfort as soon as possible. Greatness and average can't play on the same team. **What team will you play for?**

CHAPTER 10

B.F.F

(The Friends You Keep)

CHAPTER 10

BFF... (Friends you keep)

"You are the sum total of the five people you spend the most time with." Jim Rohn

Having friends who are constantly challenging and calling you out on your bull is an important aspect of making it from the streets of your fears to the stage of your dreams. We all have two friends in our group. First where's that reassuring friend you call to vent and complain because he/she will listen and agree with everything you say. Next there is that friend who almost knows you better than you know yourself. He/she has no problem disagreeing with you and telling you the truth about yourself. You avoid them because their honesty reflects back what you already know to be true.

My best friend growing up was my main man, Bryan, a.k.a "Hickman the Hitman." Our struggles were similar, we played the same sports, and we had many of the same dreams and aspirations. We were trouble wherever we went and any class we had together the teacher separated us almost immediately! We snuck off to parties and ditched classes to go to the basketball courts. Aside from all the trouble we got into, we always told each other the truth. When he had relationship trouble in high school (which happened way too often), he avoided talking to me. He would ask another friend because I would be quick to tell him if he was wrong. He was my best friend and telling him the truth was what friends do. Now don't get me wrong, he would get on me in a heartbeat! I had a bad habit of slacking and being lazy, especially in sports. If I slacked on a play, he wouldn't hesitate to curse me out! He would call me out whenever we worked out together and I did less than he knew I was capable of. But, at the end of the day, we had each other's back. We constantly challenged each other and held each other accountable.

Surrounding yourself with the right friends can help you out tremendously! Learn to have friends who lift you up rather than keep you down. Learn to have friends that build you up when you're broken down not friends that encourage you to remain the same. "You've changed" is a phrase I'm sure you have heard over the years. More often than not, it's an attempt to insult you because you're not the way that people remember you. I hope that when you hear, "you've changed", it brings a huge smile to your face. If you've been setting goals and working on yourself constantly, you should have changed! Who you were last year should be a shell of the person you are now. Too many people refuse to work on themselves and, thus, remain the same. When your friends see that you're moving on up in life and accomplishing your dreams it makes them feel insecure. You are a painful reminder of possibilities that they have yet to achieve.

Only your closest friends will celebrate with you. The right friends will be happier for your success than you are! They will look at your change as encouragement and motivation for themselves. These are the kind of friends you want and need in your life. Here is something else you should know: the more you succeed the smaller that circle of friends will get. As you grow, you'll start to notice some things about these "friends." Your tolerance for drama and nonsense won't be what it was because the person you are now won't allow that. I have had to separate myself over the years from friends that I love dearly because we chose different paths. I have learned that you'll end up with maybe two or three lifetime friends. Everyone else will be friends from your current circumstances. You will have more colleagues and associates than friends. Of course, there is nothing wrong with this and, in time, you will find that it is actually better this way.

CLEAN OUT YOUR CLOSET: The late speaker and author Jim Rohn once said "You are the sum total of the five people you spend the most time with." I have to agree with this from personal experience. As I became interested in personal development and really started applying myself, I realized that I was becoming like the people with whom I spent the most time. The way they spoke, the shows they watched, and even the places where they chilled became my places. As my priorities changed, I realized that I had to surround myself with people who were doing what I wanted to do. I needed to be around people who had the same level desire for success.

So here is my challenge to you: *clean out your closet and get some new friends*! Look at the contacts in your phone. I'm sure you could erase some numbers in there! There are a few people in your phone who always call you with drama and who just suck the energy right out of you! What about the people who only call when they need something, but they are unavailable when you ask for a favor? *ERASE THOSE NUMBERS NOW!* You don't have time for people who don't support you or encourage your growth. Get rid of them and start adding people to your circle who can help you get to the next level - people who are positive and are always striving for the best. Those kinds of people help build you up instead of break you down. Remember quality over quantity. So clean out your closet, throw out those old, ragged, smelly clothes that don't fit you anymore.

CHAPTER 11

NINJA TURTLE

(Dream Like You Mean It)

CHAPTER 11

LIKE A NINJA TURTLE... (Dream like you mean it)

"You're never given a dream without also being given the power to make it true." –Richard Bach

Everyone either has or has had a dream in their life. Some people fight to the very end to make their come true. Some give up when the adversity becomes too much. Some just never try and live life in obscurity. The importance of dreaming cannot be stressed enough. It is the beginning of all great things. Dreams are necessary to life and success. Dreams are simply plans and hopes working together. Dreams are your inner thoughts and your heart's truest desires.

The first solid dream I ever had was in Mrs. Anderson's 3rd grade class. One day the class was asked what we wanted to be when we grew up. I was the first to volunteer to share with the class and I was ready when Mrs. Anderson called my name. As I walked up to the front of class, you would think I was at runway show strutting my stuff. With my Ninja Turtle backpack, Power Rangesr t-shirt, and Spiderman light-up shoes that flashed when I walked, I was clearly the coolest 3rd grader the world has ever known. So, as I made my way to the front of the class, Mrs. Anderson asked me the single most important question you can ask a kid: "What do you want to be when you grow up?" I looked her straight in the eyes, dusted off my Power Rangers shirt, and said so convincingly, "Mrs. Anderson, I want to be the first black Teenage Mutant Ninja Turtle!" The entire classed started to laugh their butts off. Mrs. Anderson herself even laughed a little. She then asked me again and I told her once more that I wanted to be "The first black Teenage Mutant Ninja Turtle." She then asked me how I knew they weren't black? I replied as only my 3rd grade mind could - with complete honesty. "First of all they're green so that means they're not black. Then their names are Michangelo, Leonardo, Donatello, and

Raphael, and black people don't have names like that." She was so completely taken aback by my response that she had no choice but to accept my dream and then ask the next kid his.

Now, that was obviously a ridiculous dream and was impossible to achieve. But, my conviction was so strong that my teacher had to give up on convincing me otherwise. That is how we must be when in pursuit of our goals! If the dream is big enough then the adversity will always seem small. Facts, opinions of others, and statistics, mean nothing when your dream is big.

APPROACH YOUR DREAM LIKE YOU WANT TO BE A NINJA TURTLE: No matter how big your dream is, if you believe in it enough, others will believe in it, too. What matters is how much you believe it is possible. The more belief you have in yourself and your dream, the less it matters what others think about it. Dreams are just dreams until you take action and make it a reality. Bust out your Ninja Turtle-like Kung Fu moves and fight against the villain called doubt.

I want you to write down your dream with as much description as possible: what it looks like, how it feels, who will be with you, where you will be next. Don't think about how long it will take, the money you will need, the schooling you will need, the adversity you will face, or if it has ever been done. **All I want you to do is write it down then read it out loud to yourself.** You will be amazed at just how great you feel when you once again believe that anything is possible, even being a black Teenage Mutant Ninja Turtle.

CHAPTER 12

PLAN B FOR WHAT

(Never Quit)

CHAPTER 12

PLAN B FOR WHAT? (Never quit)

"Thinking realistic is the most commonly traveled road to mediocrity." –Will Smith

While living in group homes separated from my younger brothers, I didn't see the point in living. Many times I wish I had been aborted because it was obvious my birth was a terrible mistake. After all, I was a product of a one night stand conceived in a hotel room by a man who doesn't know I exist and a mother who would later abandon me. I often wondered how the world would be if my mother had taken a Plan B morning after pill? These were the questions that played over and over in the back of my mind.

After a few years of counseling and a few people showing me unconditional love, I learned that life is worth living. Once my mental issues were worked out and my confidence was gained, I was relieved that my mother didn't take that pill. I found that life is a gift that you repay by pursing your dreams. This is why I never believed in the idea of having a "Plan B" or a "back up plan" when it comes to chasing your dreams. "Plan A," is the one plan you need if you want something bad enough.

What is a Plan B anyway? What is a backup plan? To most people, it is something everyone with a dream should have. It's like an insurance plan for your dreams. When you get in a head-on collision with life, Plan B is your insurance, roadside assistance, and Enterprise Rent-a-Car to pick you up. It is comforting to know that if Plan A fails, then Plan B is waiting to step up and get in the game. But should we give up on Plan A when adversity hits? Or is there a way to always have Plan A be Plan A?

Plan A is your dream, your goal, your main plan to accomplish what you want in life. The problem with Plan A (which is why we're told we need a Plan B) is that very few of us have a clearly defined and well-planned Plan A. Because of this lack of clarity, we sound crazy when we speak of our dreams! We share enthusiastically with everyone we know about our great aspirations of becoming a pro athlete, a pop star, the President, or the next Mark Zukerberg! We speak of great things that few people dare to even imagine! Most of us don't know why we want it and, therefore, often we fail to make a well-thought-out plan to pursue these dreams. Those who love us (and those who would like us to fail) are then unable to see our vision, which forces them to offer up a safer and more realistic route to success.

If you want your "Plan A" to be the only plan you ever need, then you need to know your stuff! Having a dream comes easy. Success is sold separately! You must become a student ready to learn everything you need to know about your craft. Use whatever classes, training, books, and mentors you can learn from! When you dedicate yourself fully to your "Plan A", you realize that the plan will evolve and change. As you get new information, your first version of Plan A will not be your last.

Plan A for me growing up was to be a NBA superstar! I believed getting to the NBA was the ultimate Plan A that would make my life perfect. There was nothing you could say to persuade me that I wasn't going to be the next Lebron James. As you can imagine, I am not the next Lebron James. Following the advice of my foster dad's and my teacher, I fell back on my Plan B: to go to college and work from there. What I would later discover after college and after a couple years in the "real world," was that the NBA should never have been my Plan A. Not because the odds of playing in the NBA were so small, but because the NBA wasn't my ultimate goal. Being financially well-off, in a beautiful home, driving a fancy car, and supporting my family was my Plan A. The NBA was the only way I thought I could achieve that at the time. I was unaware of the other available options to achieve my true Plan A!

MAKE YOUR GOALS INTO AN iPHONE! Stop thinking in terms of Plan B. Instead think of your major goal in life as an iPhone. The iPhone is always and has always been the iPhone. It may change shape or color but it's still the iPhone. When there is a problem or glitch, the phone upgrades its programs from 2.0 to 2.1 and so on. Until eventually you go from the iPhone 5 to the iPhone 6. The same goes for your ultimate goal in life. Your Plan A should be your main goal in life. It is your iPhone. You don't need a backup plan but you need to adjust and upgrade as you go along. As you hit obstacles, you will upgrade your plans from Plan A 2.0 to Plan A 2.1 and so on. With new obstacles, information, and skills you will naturally change the way you accomplish your goal. Never go with plan B out of fear! There has always been one quote that I use when talking about going after your dreams: "Never give up on a dream because of the amount of time it will take to accomplish it because the time will pass anyway." If you know what you want in life, don't let the time it takes to achieve it, people's opinions, or your fears force you to fall back on "Plan B".

CHAPTER 13

OUTSIDE THE BOX

(Limits)

CHAPTER 13

OUTSIDE THE BOX... (Limits)

"There is no box, except the ones we create for ourselves." – Monti Washington

Growing up poor, I lived in an environment filled with limits and boxes literally! In Phoenix, Arizona, I lived in a homeless shelter called the Overflow for one summer. "The Overflow" was an overnight shelter for men and women. The shelter functioned like this: a big white unmarked bus that smelled like death itself picked you up at 5:30 p.m. near at this dusty field. This bus then took you to an old abandoned hanger where they fed you and gave you a place to rest overnight. One side of the shelter was for women and children and the other side for men. Different organizations and churches fed us from night to night. Sometimes we would get a hot meal and other times, all we would get was a cold sandwich and potato chips would all.

In the morning, that same white bus dropped you off at that same dusty field at 5:30 a.m. During this time my mother was at the lowest point of her drug addiction. From the moment the bus dropped off my two younger brothers and me, my mother would disappear. We would not see her until later in the evening when the bus came to pick us up. This all happened during the summer days in Phoenix, Arizona, where temperatures reached triple digits daily. In addition, this field was not only grassless, but often littered with broken beer bottles, crack pipes, and syringes.

Early that summer I caught the flu. I had no one to look after me and nor did I have a bed to rest in. This forced me to think outside the box. I wound up dumpster-diving behind a grocery store to find the biggest cardboard box available. I took that box, broke it down, and slept on it in the shade behind a soup kitchen. After a few hours, my two younger brothers woke me up when they thought a guy was trying to steal my box. Ready to defend ourselves, the guy then said he would give me $1 for it. Without hesitation, I gave the guy my box and got food with that $1. Now a dollar may not be a lot to most people, but when you're a 10-year-old homeless kid, $1 is life changing. After I was given that $1, I was hit with an idea that redefined the concept of, "Thinking Outside the Box."

The next morning, when the white bus dropped us off at the field and my mother left, I went dumpster diving. Instead of getting just one box, I got six of them. I went back to the field and started selling boxes to other homeless people for a quarter, dollar, whatever little bit of cash they had. This went on all summer. Every morning at 5:30 a.m. I would go into the trash can, get boxes, then sell them. I made anywhere from $5 to $10 a day. My younger brothers and I survived while learning how to turn a disadvantage into an advantage. We went from homeless and sleeping in boxes to selling boxes.

Thinking outside the box is how you turn a disadvantage into an advantage! It is how problems with no solution are solved. Desperation often forces us to solve problems creatively. It is a great motivator that has helped solve problems when normal means fail. Our fears prevent us from thinking outside the box. This comfort zone that we all love to stay in pretends to shield us from our fears when, in fact, it keeps us close to them. Most people cannot "Think Outside the Box" until a situation forces them to get creative. I would have never gotten the idea of taking trash and selling it to survive if my circumstances had not forced me to do so. Being open to thinking differently is what will help you get outside this "box" many of us live in.

How we got into the box is not all that complicated. It is simply from years of conditioning and learning in the most stagnant and non-creative ways possible. At a young age we were taught to think inside of the box, taught to avoid obstacles at all costs, taught to go with the crowd and blend in by not only thinking but living inside the box, There was a study done by Human Potential Expert, Herb Otto that found that one out of every 110 people look at a situation and see how something can be done; the other 109 look at things and think how it can't be done. They are conditioned to look only at the problem and not the solution. They automatically think inside the box, preventing them from finding a creative solution to their problems. It's your job to train yourself to look for new ways to solve old problems.

JUMP OUT OF THAT BOX: The last step to thinking outside the box is literally getting outside of the box. Think differently, creatively, and clearly change your surroundings. Break your routine of working at the same place, same office, and same classroom. Don't listen to music, text on your phone, watch TV, or play on the computer all day. Those distractions keep you in your box. You have to attend class, you have to work, and there are certain routines that you can't break in life. But you can change them and do them differently. This may help you **discover new life in your old life.** The day-to-day grind can get redundant and lifeless. By jumping out of your box, you have the chance to breathe new life into your life. For every problem there is a solution. That solution lies outside the box, away from your fears, and inside your creativity.

CHAPTER 14

HARD WORK STINKS

(Ask for Help)

CHAPTER 14

HARD WORK STINKS… (Ask for help)

"Don't work harder, work smarter." - Scrooge McDuck

Let's keep it real for a second: **NO ONE WANTS TO WORK HARD!** Working hard is no fun and it takes a lot of time away from doing things we want to do. We are taught that the harder we work, the more successful we'll become. **NOT ENTIRELY TRUE!** That is only one part of what it takes to be successful. Hard work only pays off when you do it in conjunction with a couple of other things. Hard work will help you become successful, but alone it will not make you successful.

Along with hard work you need a sufficient amount of knowledge about what you're pursuing. But the attainment of that knowledge still isn't enough because knowledge isn't power, applied knowledge is power! You can study as hard as you want for that final exam, but if you're studying the wrong chapters and not applying what you know, YOU'RE STILL GOING TO FAIL THE TEST! **It's not enough to simply know what to do - knowing how to do it correctly is what matters most!**

In the book, *Outliers* by Malcolm Gladwell, there is a chapter on the "10,000 hours" theory. Long story short: it was found that in order to achieve true greatness in any area of life, all that it took was "10,000 hours of practice. Everyone from Bill Gates, The Beatles, Mozart and so on, all had that in common. During those 10,000 hours, each one of them had to face the adversity of hard work. Bill Gates, from the time he was in middle school, spent well over 10,000 hours in front of a computer. The Beatles performed well over 10,000 hours before the British invasion landed in the U.S. Mozart was a child prodigy, but his greatest work wasn't created until later in his adult years (after 10,000 hours of practice). What was the "X factor" in their success? **It was their ability to do things correctly for a sustained period of time.**

I know, I know - I just blew your mind away with that. It's ok, take your time and catch your breath. 10,000 hours of working hard and making sure you're doing it correctly? Sounds a little crazy now, doesn't it? Well, it's not only crazy it's worth it! It is a level of dedication unimaginable for the average person. Because you're reading this book and taking the time to better yourself, I don't believe that you are an average person. Successful people do things the right way! **Doing things the right way always gets you the right results. Is hard work essential to success? Absolutely! Just don't be fooled into thinking that's all it takes to be successful!**

ASK FOR HELP! No one is stupid or dumb. Some people simply don't know what they don't know. My adversity tip for you is to ask for help. Seek out mentors and experts to help you learn to do things the right way. Chances are that whatever you're trying to achieve, someone else out there has already done it. Why spin your wheels and make hundreds of mistakes when you can find people who have already made those mistakes and simply learn from them? Work hard AND smart at finding these people. They will save you a lot of time and unnecessary hard work by showing you **THE RIGHT WAY** to do things.

CHAPTER 15

FAIL LIKE YOU MEAN IT

(All Part of the Game)

CHAPTER 15

Fail Like you Mean It!.. (All Part of the Game)

"Failure is an event, not a person." –Zig Ziglar

Early on in my life I was made to believe that I was a complete and utter failure. My first foster parents reminded me on a regular basis of this fact anytime I attempted to do anything. Being reminded of your mother giving you up for drugs and being in Special Ed classes did not help my confidence or self-esteem. I truly believed I was a failure in every sense of the word. That is, until I discovered that just because someone thinks you're a failure does not mean it's true. I realized that I am a success and not a failure, as long as I never give up and continue going after my dreams.

Failure is the mask that hides success. On your journey to success, failure will meet you and shake your hand. It will ask you out on a date and even pay for the bill. It will invite you over to watch a movie and ask you to stay the night. It will cuddle with you, watch the game next to you, and try to make you as comfortable as possible. Failure wants to eventually marry you and start a family with you. It wants you to live in this house called "comfort zone." It wants to have three kids and name them Mediocrity, Settling, and Regret.

Failure has a way disguising itself as "The end." It has this way of making you believe that it is all over and that you should quit. Don't fall for it! Failure is nothing more than **SUCCESS TURNED INSIDE OUT.** We learn the most from our failures. When we fail at something we have not lost. We have simply found a way that does not work! It is our responsibility to keep at it until we get what we want. **If you're failing then you're growing. Failure means you're trying something new and taking risks in life.** It takes great courage to fail over and over again. The same courage it takes to fail is the same courage needed to convert adversity into success.

Failure doesn't stand in your way of success. Accepting it and blaming others is what will get in your way. You can fail your way to the top! Many successful people in life have done just that. Michael Jordan has missed over 3,000 shots in his career, but all you remember are the ones he made. Jack Canfield (co-creator of the *Chicken Soup for the Soul* series) took the first book to more than 100 publishers before someone finally took a chance on it. It is now one of the best-selling book series of all time. Failure and success are the two best friends you will ever have. One helps you learn; the other gives you confidence.

BECOME A PROFESSIONAL FAILURE! Fail every chance that you get. But, when you fail, fail, and then fail better! Give everything you have into what you're trying to accomplish by going "Ollin" with no worries about the outcome. With each failure try not to repeat the same mistake in the same way. Learn from your previous mistakes and failures so that you don't get stuck because you didn't learn the lesson. Great failure is usually followed by great success. As you continue to grow and fail, you will discover, just as I did, that, "There are no failures in life, only lessons."

CHAPTER 16

MAN THOSE STINK

(No More Excuses)

CHAPTER 16

MAN THOSE STINK… (No More Excuses)

"Excuses are merely nails used to build a house a failure"- Habeeb Akande

My high school basketball coach loved to talk. He would give speeches even when it wasn't necessary. Half of our practice time was spent listening to him, while the other half was spent trying NOT to listen to him. Nevertheless, he was an amazing coach a and great role model. The one thing coach did not tolerate was excuses. He did not give them or accept them. With him, it was better to just say "Yes, Sir" and "No, Sir" rather than give an excuse for why you were late to practice. For every excuse, he would give you a 10-minute speech. Every speech would end with the same quote: **"Excuses are like butts, everyone has one and they all stink."**

Excuses are like parachutes with holes in them. It may look like that parachute will stop you from falling, but before you know it you're falling faster than before. We use excuses to justify putting forth less effort. They are the soft pillows on the beds of failure. Remember that failure is a part of life, as are setbacks, problems, challenges, and obstacles. When you make excuses, you throw away the opportunity to GROW through it rather than just GO through it. Excuses give you a false sense of security and accomplishment while keeping you in your comfort zone, stopping you from ever reaching your full potential! When we take responsibility and discard our excuses, we learn what we need to improve. Learning and growth are essential in making it from the streets of your fears to the stage of your dreams.

OWN UP TO YOUR EVERY MISTAKE! When you find yourself about to make an excuse, simply pause and think about why you are making the excuse. Think of what that says about your character. Ask yourself: Will people trust me? Does this make me dependable? How will this excuse help me find success? You will discover quickly that **excuses don't help you turn adversity into success; they turn you away from it.** Even if you make mistakes and occasionally fail, when you own your failures rather than make excuses, growth takes place and enables you to turn adversity into success!

CHAPTER 17

MAKE UP YOUR MIND

(Make a Decision)

CHAPTER 17

MAKE UP YOUR MIND MAN... (Make a Decision)

"Success is a choice. Happiness is a decision." Unknown

Your decisions in life are what truly define who and what you are. Despite the limitations of my childhood, I made decisions that allowed me to avoid becoming just "another statistic." Unfortunately, many people with my background fall short of a happy, successful life because of their circumstances. My best friend, my little brother, is defined by the decision he made to engage in illegal activities. He is now serving seven years in prison and will be branded a felon the rest of his life. We both experienced the same pain, disappointment, and hardships. The difference was our perspective on our experiences and the choices we made.

Perception is key to making decisions in tough situations. **What you perceive, you will believe.** If you believe the problem is a threat, then that is what it will be. If you see it as an opportunity to grow, then you will grow. Your perception of the situation makes it easier for you to make the right decision. Facts are facts! We cannot change what happened to us or wish that it never happened. This isn't the Wizard of Oz where we can just click our heels three times! We're not in Kansas anymore, Dorothy! This is real life with real issues. There is nothing more real than your perception of any given situation.

I once viewed optimists as annoying people living in a fairy tale. I cannot stress to you just how much I disliked those people! They seemed naïve as well as in denial of reality. I later discovered that optimists simply had a greater perception of the bigger picture. They decided not to let their adversity deter them from seeing the big picture. With the right perception, your decision making skills improve from top to bottom. Rather than thinking that a late arrival to class will ruin your life, you can now see that being late to class is simply being late to class. An optimistic perspective further helps your decision making ability.

CHANGE YOUR CONTACT LENSES: Work daily on changing your perspective on adversity. Doing this will greatly improve your decision making skills. You can look at your options clearly based off the information and evidence at hand. Think back to the hardest decision you've ever made. Did you make the decision out of fear or love? Were you worrying about all of its possible negative outcomes? Or were you optimistic in the face of that adversity? These questions will help you discover the truth of decision making under pressure. The truth you will find is that the contact lenses you use will determine the quality of the decision you've made. **WAS IT BLURRY WITH WORRY? OR CLEAR OF FEAR?**

CHAPTER 18

WALK THE WALK

(Taking Action)

CHAPTER 18

WALK THE WALK... (Taking Action)

"The successful person has the habit of doing the things failures don't like to do." -Unknown

Being in Special Education classes while my friends were in general classes made me feel like the world's biggest failure. I was the guy in the classroom that everyone laughed at when it was time to read. To say I wasn't a good reader is as much of an understatement as I can make. I believed that I was too stupid to read an entire page without getting half the words wrong. I had zero confidence in myself because of the abuse I suffered in some of my foster homes. It wasn't until I started to take action that I began catching up to everyone else. I was constantly being tutored and going to after school programs. I was not afraid to ask for help. It was *THE ACTION I TOOK* that allowed me to go from taking special education classes to being an honor roll student!

Taking action is essential to achieving success. Act on all your dreams and goals. What you do matters more than what you think or say. Your actions reveal what you are, who you are, and what you represent. Your dreams, goals, and aspirations in life will never be more than that, unless you act on them. It is in consistent action that dreams become a reality. No matter how many times you fail, you must continue to act. You must not allow your emotions, feelings, or others' opinions stop you from taking the actions to get what you want out of life.

When do people hesitate to take action on their dreams? When the fear is greater than the passion. The only way to overcome that fear is to take action on whatever fear is preventing you from moving forward. There is nothing wrong with acknowledging the fact that fear is indeed present. Admitting that you're afraid to move forward takes strength that most people don't have. But once you admit your fears, you can begin to work through them. That is how you learn that the fear is nothing more than your imagination working negatively. Fear is not real! It is your imagination working with your past to create obstacles that may not even exist. You must take action to move toward your goals. Abraham Lincoln said, "Things may come to those who wait, but only the things left by those who hustle." (Maybe I paraphrased a bit but you get the idea)

WORK, DON'T TALK! Don't hesitate to take the first step of action. The longer you wait, hesitate, and procrastinate, the longer you allow fear to take over. **TODAY I WANT YOU TO TAKE ACTION ON YOUR #1 GOAL IN LIFE!** Walk, don't talk! Gain experience along the way. Remember, experience is the best teacher there is. No amount of thinking, planning, or talking will replace simply taking action! Once you get a basic plan down and gather all of your resources **GO FOR IT!** Don't fall into the trap of **WAITING FOR THE RIGHT MOMENT!** The right moment is the moment you take action! The right moment is when you get off your butt, on your feet, and get moving. Will Smith said it best in the movie *The Pursuit of Happiness*, "If you want something, go get it. Period!"

CHAPTER 19

TO GROW OR NOT TO GROW
(Growth)

CHAPTER 19

To Grow or Not To Grow, That Is The Question? (Growth)

"Don't just *go* through it, *grow* through it." –Monti Washington

Success is a choice, happiness is a choice, and growth is also a choice. When asked how I made it from the streets to the stage, I say it was because I made a choice. I made a choice to "grow" through my problems and not simply "go" through my problems. Now, granted, my last foster parents helped me understand what family was; Vicki and Jeffery Banks taught me many lessons that helped me get here. There were many others who helped along the way, but in the end I made a choice. I made the hard choice to grow and see my situation as a way to "drive" me and not to "destroy" me.

The essence of success is growth. The only way to grow is to change. The only way to change into who we want to be is to learn. Unfortunately, the problem with growth is that it's optional. We can't help but to change, but growth is a choice. It forces you to leave who you were to become who you are. It forces you to face the sides of yourself that are holding you back from growing into the person you were meant to be. This scares most people because we're afraid of our own greatness. We get so use to our comfort zone and playing small that we forget the need to grow. We forget that when we stretch ourselves or accomplish a goal we set, we experience true joy and happiness.

We all know that life can be a Bi*ch! People die unexpectedly. Best friends stab us in the back. Family can turn into enemies. There are all these horrible things life throws at us when we least expect it. This is exactly why growing is so important! When devastating situations occur, growth helps drive you when it would normally destroy you. Bad things happen to good people! Life will punch you in the face even if you don't deserve it! Growing up I didn't deserve to be abused and hospitalized but life hit me with a curve ball. Life may throw you curve balls that you can't hit. Constant growth will help you deal and cope with these issues, turning your greatest pain into your greatest strength.

BECOME ADDICTED TO GROWTH! I want you to be a growth addict! Constantly seek out new ways that challenge you to grow. There is no greater challenge than the challenge to improve yourself. In the next month, read a book. Read a book that is specific to your major or in the same field as the dream you want to achieve in life. Whatever the area in which you want to make lots of money, invest in a book. Build the habit of reading, watching, and learning everything there is to know about your field. To earn a Ph.D. you need to read 38-52 books in your area of study in order to write a dissertation. There are 52 weeks in the year, if you read a book a week for an entire year, you would have technically earned a Ph.D. Decide right now if your dream, your happiness, the impact you can have on this world, is worth growing and becoming your best for. If so, then start by learning all there is to know about your dream and goals.

CHAPTER 20

LIFE OR DEATH

(Your Life Depends On it)

CHAPTER 20

LIFE OR DEATH... (Your life depends on it)

"Success is not final, Failure is not fatal." -anonymous

Tedai Buddhist Monks in China choose to take on a quest known as the Kaihogyo. They believe that to achieve enlightenment in your current life you must take on a 1,000 day challenge over a seven year period. The quest goes as follows:

- Years 1-3 monks run 18 miles a day for 100 straight days
- YEAR 4 -5 monks run 18 miles a day for 200 straight days
- After year 5, they have to for 9 days not eat, drink water, or sleep
- YEAR 6 - monks run 37 miles a day for 100 straight days
- YEAR 7 - monks run 52 miles per day for 100 straight days and 18 miles a day for the final 100 days

For the record, I am not a Tedai Monk and will not be attempting the Kaihogyo. If your smart neither should you! But there were many times growing up when I was faced with life or death situations. Seeing my mother physically abused by her boyfriends forced me to intervene several times, putting my own life in danger. Add to that the fact that I went days with nothing to eat, then you can see how I understand this "life or death" concept. Having pers onally faced life or death situations (including an attempt to take my own life), I can attest to the importan n/mce of committing yourself fully to your dreams like it is a life or death situation.

Why am telling you to approach your dreams and goals like it's life or death? Because it is! Have you ever seen someone work a job that gives them absolutely no fulfillment? What about someone who is always putting other people down because their life has no meaning? In my world, that is worse than death itself. They are not alive; they are simply trying to survive.

When I was sleeping in parks and eating leftover picnic food out of the trash can, my dream kept me going. Having goals and dreams is what allowed me to - write a book. Having a purpose and making it a life or death situation turned a kid who was in special education classes until 8th grade into a man who graduated with two degrees. **I MADE IT LIFE OR DEATH!** Not a physical but a spiritual death.

Every day we are alive we can seek out our passion, achieve our dreams, and pursue our goals. Living life without passion or fulfillment is a hard life to live. Going after your heart's greatest desires is the only way to live. Misfortune will strike along the way, often when we least expect it. On some days you will feel like a Tedai Monk running 52 miles in a single day knowing the same fate awaits you tomorrow. Remember you are on a quest! Unlike the monks, if you fail you don't have to die, you can just try again the next day.

MAKE LIFE OR DEATH DECISIONS: Make going after your dreams and goals a life or death decision. Tell yourself you need this to feel alive! Remember life is a quest with many miles to run. You will get tired and feel like you want to stop your quest and live below your potential. Summon up the courage and the commitment to hold fast to your dreams. Conviction and commitment are key! In the 400 years of the Kaihogyo only 46 monks have completed the quest. Lace up your shoes and get to running!

TIME TO GET MONTIVATED!
(20-day challenge)

It's time to take action and turn your adversity into success! Now is the time to take the 20 lessons you have learned in reading this book and put them into motion. I have shared with you my many struggles, ranging from being abused in foster home after foster home, to eating out of trash cans, to being in Special Ed classes until 8th grade. These were the lessons I learned along the way that helped me make it from the streets of my fears to standing proudly on the stage of my dreams.

We all have a story that is filled with our personal brand of adversity that we must learn to turn into success. I hope that by reading this book you now have a starting point or more inspiration to keep striving to achieve whatever success means to you. It's not easy to find the light when it feels like our life is covered by darkness. Oftentimes, the only choice we believe we have left is to quit. I encourage you not to quit and, choose to keep fighting. Regardless of your circumstances, if you take these 20 lessons and apply them to your daily life you will see a change in yourself and your circumstances that you never could have imagined. You will find yourself turning everyday adversity into not-so-everyday success.

Here, I have provided you with a recap of all the lessons throughout this book. Now, I want you to take the next 20 days and do your best to implement each one into your everyday life. Simply take the time to read one lesson each day and apply it to your day. This challenge is not about getting everything right and not making any mistakes. **Rather, it is about getting you to change your perspective on adversity.** At the end of the 20 days you'll see that we succeed not in spite of the adversity we face, but *because* of the adversity we face. You will be able to use the adversity you face not as a crutch for your excuses, but instead as a *catapult* for your achievements.

DAY 1

FIND YOUR "WHY?" Find a reason so strong that there are no obstacles strong enough in the world to stop you. This "why" needs to be something that affects you emotionally every time you think of it. It can be a dream, family member, loved one who passed away, anything that gives you the strength to move forward. The key is to choose this "why" from an emotional standpoint. Money, cars, or big houses are rarely strong enough reasons to make it through extreme situations. Your "why" should make you feel unstoppable when you think about it!

DAY 2

FOCUS EVERYTHING YOU HAVE ON ONE PARTICULAR GOAL. It can be to get better grades, be in a healthy relationship, get that internship secured, get your own place, or get in the best shape of your life. **For the next month I want you to focus on ways to improve that area and everyday take action on making it better.** Let your mind think of every possible way to achieve the goal without limiting yourself. Write it down where you will see it everyday. You should read it when you go to bed and when you wake up in the morning. You want to create the habit of focusing on this one goal. At the end of the month you will be surprised at how much you're able to accomplish with 100% of your focus. You will not worry about how green someone else's grass is, because you'll have the best lawn on the block.

DAY 3

GIVE THE RIGHT WORDS POWER! Use words that empower you every time you speak them. Phrases such as "I can't", "I give up", "I didn't think", "I'm afraid of", "It's impossible", and "I don't believe" are words that steal power. Have **"POWER WORDS"** and **"SUCCESS PHRASES"** such as, "I expect", "I believe", "it's possible", or "I'll find a way!"   Allow the words you use to empower you to accomplish incredible feats. In his book "**ASPIRE**" Kevin Hall talks about the immense power of words.   He writes about. "Ollin," pronounced "all in," which means to "move and act now with all your heart."   It's a powerful word that I try to use in everyday life.   Learn to use these words to replace those that steal your energy. Remember that sticks and stones may break bones, but words leaves scars.

DAY 4

FIRST LOVE YOURSELF: Before you can F.L.Y you have to discover why you're stuck on the ground. Ask yourself, "What is holding me back?"   It could be that no one has ever taught you how to love yourself.   It could be because of a traumatic past that has robbed you of it.   YOU ARE NOT A HELPLESS VICTIM!   There are no excuses for not loving yourself.   I'm not saying that it's going to be easy, but it's necessary.   It's necessary for you to take back the power you're entitled to that comes with loving oneself.   You'll face a lot of disappointment along the way, but you should never quit. Believe me, when you're able to F.L.Y, you'll simply be able to rise above all the hardships thrown at you.   But **FIRST LOVE YOURSELF**.

DAY 5

Ketchup to your past: Think back to a tough time in your life. Maybe it was an life-changing injury, your parents' divorce, a lack of money, issues with close friends, or self-esteem issues.   Now think about how that made you feel. Does it bring you down?   Does it fill you with regret?   If it does, look at it from a different perspective.   See it as something you survived, overcame, defeated, rather than something that has held you back.   Our past is how we see it.   You can see your struggles as a disadvantage or an advantage.   Ketchup to your past!   Go backwards to move forward!

Recalling those tough times allows you to see what was holding you back from having the present and future that you want. The key is to reflect **NOT** dwell on the past.

My friends always laugh at me because I always carry a ketchup package in my pocket. The ketchup package in my pocket that I carry every day is a reminder of what I have overcome. What is your Ketchup package? What do you have that can remind you just how strong you really are? What do you have that reminds you of just how powerful and amazing you really are? Take a picture of it, keep a memory of it, or, if possible, carry it with you. Life is always changing and we never know what is coming our way. When our present looks bad, and our dreams look impossible, we have our past to remind us just how far we have come. **Ketchup** to your past only to **relish** in the moment!

DAY 6

BECOME AN ENTREPRENEUR! Life will give you many lemons, each one with that sour taste. You can choose to make lemonade out of it and simply turn it into a lesson. Or, you can take the lessons and turn it into something **more.** Turn it into something that will benefit you and others for the rest of your life. There is an opportunity in every difficulty. Our world desperately needs problem-solvers and creative people with minds like yours. Ask yourself, "What problems am I good at solving?" "Who else has these problems?" And, "How can I solve their problems?" When you become great at solving problems for people, they will pay you for it! Not only are you helping them, but you are helping yourself in the process.

DAY 7

MAKE THE DEALER RESHUFFLE! From now on, accept nothing but the best. Do not settle for less when you know you deserve more. Whether it's a job, relationship, friendship, or the relationship with yourself! Create a mindset that allows you to play every hand you are dealt to the best of your ability. When you feel like you are being treated unfairly, speak up! When you feel you can do more, then do more! Demand of yourself the best life has to offer. When you learn how to convert adversity into success, you will no longer have to play any cards you're dealt. You'll be in a position to make the dealer reshuffle and give you the cards you want!

DAY 8

LAUGH OUT LOUD. When you're faced with a situation that is out of your control, just laugh out loud. Laugh, giggle, snicker, do whatever you have to do to PRESS THE PAUSE BUTTON ON YOUR THOUGHTS. Sometimes things get so messed up and out of our control that we have no choice but to laugh! In that moment being stressed out or panicking will only make things worse. By laughing out loud you are telling your mind and body to calm down and just relax. You are altering your mental and physical state which allows you to see the problem for what it is and not what you make it to be. Watch something funny on YouTube that makes absolutely no sense! No matter how ridiculous it may sound, laugh your butt off! When you feel better, you will see the situation for what it is and not what you make it to be.

DAY 9

BE A LOVER NOT A FIGHTER! I know what you're thinking, "Excuse me tall, bald, black man, what do you mean be a lover not a fighter? When people love what they do, they normally excel at it. The dancer will practice nine hours a day until she gets a move down. An aspiring doctor will attend school for 10 years or more just earn the title of doctor. An Olympic sprinter will train six hours a day for four years, all for a 10 second race. When you love what you do, it hurts to be average. It hurts not to be the best after all of your hard work. On the other hand, when you do things you don't like, you fight it. You fight getting to that class you hate. You fight getting out of bed for the job that you truly dislike. When you Love what you do, you don't have to worry or even consider being average. They enjoy the challenge and every adversity that comes their way. Doing what you love prevents you from being average because most people don't do what they love. They do what "most" people do: settle and find comfort as soon as possible. Greatness and average can't play on the same team. **What team will you play for?**

DAY 10

CLEAN OUT YOUR CLOSET: The late speaker and author Jim Rohn once said "You are the sum total of the five people you spend the most time with." I have to agree with this from personal experience. As I became interested in personal development and really started applying myself, I realized that I was becoming like the people with whom I spent the most time. The way they spoke, the shows they watched, and even the places where they chilled became my places. As my priorities changed, I realized that I had to surround myself with people who were doing what I wanted to do. I needed to be around people who had the same level desire for success.

So here is my challenge to you: *clean out your closet and get some new friends*! Look at the contacts in your phone. I'm sure you could erase some numbers in there! There are a few people in your phone who always call you with drama and who just suck the energy right out of you! What about the people who only call when they need something, but they are unavailable when you ask for a favor? *ERASE THOSE NUMBERS NOW!* You don't have time for people who don't support you or encourage your growth. Get rid of them and start adding people to your circle who can help you get to the next level - people who are positive and are always striving for the best. Those kinds of people help build you up instead of break you down. Remember quality over quantity. So clean out your closet, throw out those old, ragged, smelly clothes that don't fit you anymore.

DAY 11

APPROACH YOUR DREAM LIKE YOU WANT TO BE A NINJA TURTLE: No matter how big your dream is, if you believe in it enough, others will believe in it, too. What matters is how much you believe it is possible. The more belief you have in yourself and your dream, the less it matters what others think about it. Dreams are just dreams until you take action and make it a reality. Bust out your Ninja Turtle-like Kung Fu moves and fight against the villain called doubt.

I want you to write down your dream with as much description as possible: what it looks like, how it feels, who will be with you, where you will be next. Don't think about how long it will take, the money you will need, the schooling you will need, the adversity you will face, or if it has ever been done. **All I want you to do is write it down then read it out loud to yourself.** You will be amazed at just how great you feel when you once again believe that anything is possible, even being a black Teenage Mutant Ninja Turtle.

DAY 12

MAKE YOUR GOALS INTO AN iPHONE! Stop thinking in terms of Plan B. Instead think of your major goal in life as an iPhone. The iPhone is always and has always been the iPhone. It may change shape or color but it's still the iPhone. When there is a problem or glitch, the phone upgrades its programs from 2.0 to 2.1 and so on. Until eventually you go from the iPhone 5 to the iPhone 6. The same goes for your ultimate goal in life. Your Plan A should be your main goal in life. It is your iPhone. You don't need a backup plan but you need to adjust and upgrade as you go along. As you hit obstacles, you will upgrade your plans from Plan A 2.0 to Plan A 2.1 and so on. With new obstacles, information, and skills you will naturally change the way you accomplish your goal. Never go with plan B out of fear! There has always been one quote that I use when talking about going after your dreams: "Never give up on a dream because of the amount of time it will take to accomplish it because the time will pass anyway." If you know what you want in life, don't let the time it takes to achieve it, people's opinions, or your fears force you to fall back on "Plan B".

DAY 13

JUMP OUT OF THAT BOX: The last step to thinking outside the box is literally getting outside of the box. Think differently, creatively, and clearly change your surroundings. Break your routine of working at the same place, same office, and same classroom. Don't listen to music, text on your phone, watch TV, or play on the computer all day. Those distractions keep you in your box. You have to attend class, you have to work, and there are certain routines that you can't break in life. But you can change them and do them differently. This may help you **discover new life in your old life.** The day-to-day grind can get redundant and lifeless. By jumping out of your box, you have the chance to breathe new life into your life. For every problem there is a solution. That solution lies outside the box, away from your fears, and inside your creativity.

DAY 14

ASK FOR HELP! No one is stupid or dumb. Some people simply don't know what they don't know. My adversity tip for you is to ask for help. Seek out mentors and experts to help you learn to do things the right way. Chances are that whatever you're trying to achieve, someone else out there has already done it. Why spin your wheels and make hundreds of mistakes when you can find people who have already made those mistakes and simply learn from them? Work hard AND smart at finding these people. They will save you a lot of time and unnecessary hard work by showing you **THE RIGHT WAY** to do things.

DAY 15

BECOME A PROFESSIONAL FAILURE! Fail every chance that you get. But, when you fail, fail, and then fail better! Give everything you have into what you're trying to accomplish by going "Ollin" with no worries about the outcome. With each failure try not to repeat the same mistake in the same way. Learn from your previous mistakes and failures so that you don't get stuck because you didn't learn the lesson. Great failure is usually followed by great success. As you continue to grow and fail, you will discover, just as I did, that, "There are no failures in life, only lessons."

DAY 16

OWN UP TO YOUR EVERY MISTAKE! When you find yourself about to make an excuse, simply pause and think about why you are making the excuse. Think of what that says about your character. Ask yourself: Will people trust me? Does this make me dependable? How will this excuse help me find success? You will discover quickly that **excuses don't help you turn adversity into success; they turn you away from it.** Even if you make mistakes and occasionally fail, when you own your failures rather than make excuses, growth takes place and enables you to turn adversity into success!

DAY 17

CHANGE YOUR CONTACT LENSES: Work daily on changing your perspective on adversity. Doing this will greatly improve your decision making skills. You can look at your options clearly based off the information and evidence at hand. Think back to the hardest decision you've ever made. Did you make the decision out of fear or love? Were you worrying about all of its possible negative outcomes? Or were you optimistic in the face of that adversity? These questions will help you discover the truth of decision making under pressure. The truth you will find is that the contact lenses you use will determine the quality of the decision you've made. **WAS IT BLURRY WITH WORRY? OR CLEAR OF FEAR?**

DAY 18

WORK, DON'T TALK! Don't hesitate to take the first step of action. The longer you wait, hesitate, and procrastinate, the longer you allow fear to take over. **TODAY I WANT YOU TO TAKE ACTION ON YOUR #1 GOAL IN LIFE**! Walk, don't talk! Gain experience along the way. Remember, experience is the best teacher there is. No amount of thinking, planning, or talking will replace simply taking action! Once you get a basic plan down and gather all of your resources **GO FOR IT!** Don't fall into the trap of **WAITING FOR THE RIGHT MOMENT!** The right moment is the moment you take action! The right moment is when you get off your butt, on your feet, and get moving. Will Smith said it best in the movie *The Pursuit of Happiness*, "If you want something, go get it. Period!"

DAY 19

BECOME ADDICTED TO GROWTH! I want you to be a growth addict! Constantly seek out new ways that challenge you to grow. There is no greater challenge than the challenge to improve yourself. In the next month, read a book. Read a book that is specific to your major or in the same field as the dream you want to achieve in life. Whatever the area in which you want to make lots of money, invest in a book. Build the habit of reading, watching, and learning everything there is to know about your field. To earn a Ph.D. you need to read 38-52 books in your area of study in order to write a dissertation. There are 52 weeks in the year, if you read a book a week for an entire year, you would have technically earned a Ph.D. Decide right now if your dream, your happiness, the impact you can have on this world, is worth growing and becoming your best for. If so, then start by learning all there is to know about your dream and goals.

DAY 20

MAKE LIFE OR DEATH DECISIONS: Make going after your dreams and goals a life or death decision. Tell yourself you need this to feel alive! Remember life is a quest with many miles to run. You will get tired and feel like you want to stop your quest and live below your potential. Summon up the courage and the commitment to hold fast to your dreams. Conviction and commitment are key! In the 400 years of the Kaihogyo only 46 monks have completed the quest. Lace up your shoes and get to running!

ABOUT THE AUTHOR

Monti Washington is refreshingly different. His keynotes, book, and workshops are engaging, educational, and empowering! His honesty and humor keeps audiences fully engaged, while his message educates and empowers audiences with the knowledge, skills, and motivation needed to be successful in the midst of adversity.

Conceived in a hotel room, a product of a one night stand, Monti's passion for impacting lives stems from the adversity he faced early on in life. Forced to live in poverty due to his mother's drug addiction, Monti grew up sleeping in cardboard boxes, living in parks, and being abused by foster parent after foster parent. Until 8th grade Monti was in Special Ed Classes and was held back on two separate occasions.

Despite the adversity he faced, Monti would go on to obtain two college degrees, become a state basketball champion, award-winning poet, a nationally recognized actor, an author, and the co-founder of **Truality.org,** a non-profit organization aimed at inspiring youth to be TRU The Real U. Known by many to be a constant positive influence with anyone he encounters, it's no wonder Monti is requested by colleges, organizations, and conferences nation wide. As a top motivational speaker, Monti has impacted the lives of thousands all over America and is recognized as "Americas Adversity Coach" for his ability to show those he comes into contact with how to turn any adversity in life into success.

His life philosophy is to live a life of constant growth. Simply enduring the pain in our lives associated with adversity is not sufficient for happiness. He believes you mustn't just go through it, but growth through it! Understanding firsthand how harsh life can be, he encourages people to use the adversity in their lives not as a crutch for their excuses, but, rather, as a catapult for their achievements!

MESSAGE FROM THE AUTHOR

I wholeheartedly hope that the message and lessons in this book have, at the very least, helped you change your perspective on adversity. I believe that to leave who we are pretending to be so that we can become who we are destined to be takes growth. Growth cannot happen without a little resistance and struggle (i.e. adversity) The adversity I have faced in my life has shaped me into the person I am today and I wouldn't change a thing. Sleeping on a park bench, getting beaten, and even watching my mother succumb to drug addiction, are all part of the adversity I had to face to be able to write this book.

Whatever adversity you are facing in your life, understand that it is meant to build you up and not break you down. The success that you dream of in life lies on the other side of your adversity. Any complaining, excuses, self-pitying, or quitting is just wasted energy that can be used in a more constructive way. I honestly believe that without adversity there would be no success. There would be no struggle, which would make any victory an empty one. Oftentimes, when we succeed it feels amazing because we have known what failure feels like prior. Knowing that the price we paid was effort, perseverance, and pain, makes the achievement feel that much better.

Embrace adversity the same way that I have. Every day for the rest of your life Adversity will be staring you in the face. It will become your best friend, your coach, your teacher, your significant other, and more. Instead of fighting it I challenge you to embrace it. Once you embrace adversity and see it as something to drive you destroy you, there is no level of success you'll be unable to reach.

Why book Monti as your speaker at your next event?

Monti has spoken all across the United States, speaking for high schools, colleges, corporations, associations & business groups. Sharing his unique story in a way that resonates with audiences of all ages makes it impossible for you not to have a new outlook on life after hearing him speak. His ability to engage, educate, and empower audiences makes Monti a must-have keynote speaker at your next event. Recommended by college coordinators, students, educators, and organizations, you can see why he is one of the most in-demand young speakers of today.

Monti's Keynotes and Programs

From the Streets to the Stage: (Inspirational Keynote)

From the Streets to the Stage is an interactive presentation designed to entertain, engage, and empower students to make it from the streets of their fears to the stage of their dreams. Through crowd participation, storytelling, spoken word poetry and other unique forms of entertainment, students learn how to take the lessons learned in school and apply them to the outside world.

Adversity University: (Leadership program)

Class is now in session! The ability to handle adversity is essential to becoming a great leader in any organization! Monti AKA "America's Adversity Coach" shows corporations, associations, and college campuses everywhere how to turn adversity into success and become a great leader in the process.

Adversity University is an interactive keynote/workshop designed to give participants the tools needed to develop the leadership, problem solving, and creative thinking skills required to transform their organizations from good to great!

Diversity University (great for college campuses and organizations seeking a new outlook on diversity)

Diversity University is an interactive keynote and workshop breaking down the conditioning and stereotyping used to separate organizations rather than bring them together. Monti Washington and top female motivational speaker Julia Garcia team up to show college campuses and organizations that not everything is black and white! This program is designed to challenge preconceived stereotype notions while giving participants the tools to work effectively with people of varied backgrounds and cultures in their organizations and on campus.

TOP 4 REASONS EVENT COORDINATORS HIRE MONTI TO SPEAK

1. **ENAGAGING PERSONALITY**
   a. Monti's ability to engage and interact with audiences is second to none. With his acting background Monti is able to deliver a message to your audiences that will not only keep them engaged, but empower them in the process.

2. **UPLIFTING STORY**
   a. A product of a one night stand who has suffered abuse in every aspect. Monti's story is able to touch the hearts of every audience who is willing to hear his story. By sharing his personal struggle and how he was able to make it from the streets to the stage, your audiences will be inspired and motivated to turn their own **PAIN INTO POWER.**

3. **CREDIBILTY AS A SPEAKER**
   a. With endorsements from Superbowl champions (Prince Amukamara New York Giants), Top Motivational speakers (TW Walker of Super hero success, Jerome Vincent Carter of Inspiration 52) and many event coordinators and college youth foundations such as "The Right Way Foundation" (an organization helping former foster youth get jobs). It's easy to see why his credibility speaks for itself.

4. EXPERIENCE YOU CAN DEPEND ON

    a. In the last 7 years Monti has spoken to 1000's across the nation. Speaking at Universities, Conferences, for business groups and associations. You can rest assure that whatever message your audience's needs, Monti will deliver. His experience allows him to stand by his claim that "I will be the easiest speaker you have ever worked with." Understanding there is a lot that goes into making an event happen, Monti will make sure that your event will be a hit with your audiences.

FOR BOOKING FEES AND DETAILS, PLEASE CONTACT:

The Contemporary Issues Agency
809 Turnberry Drive
Waunakee, WI 53597-2256

Call Now!
800-843-2179
info@ciaspeakers.com

Made in the USA
Coppell, TX
06 March 2020

16545345R00056